ALSO BY MICHAEL PALMER

MICHAEL PALMER

COMPANY OF MOTHS

A NEW DIRECTIONS BOOK

Manufactured in the United States of America
New Directions Books are printed on acid-free paper
First published as New Directions Paperbook 1011 in 2005
Published simultaneously in Canada by Penguin Books Canada Limited

ACKNOWLEDGMENTS: Many of these poems first appeared in the following publications: *The Best American Poetry 2001; Bombay Gin; Chicago Review; Colorado Review; Conjunctions; Crossroads; Five Fingers Review; Fulcrum; Mantis; New American Writing; NO: A Journal of the Arts; PN Review; ZYZZYVA*. Broadsides were produced by: Evergreen State College; Eucalyptus Press; Pressed Wafer; The University Libraries at the State University of New York, Buffalo (with a pastel by Irving Petlin). A number of poems also appeared in the anthology *Place as Purpose. Poetry from the Western States* (eds. Martha Ronk & Paul Vangelisti, Autry Museum of Western Heritage/Sun & Moon Press). "Scale" was first published in *Richter 858* (ed. David Breskin, The Shifting Foundation: SF MOMA). The volume consists of a series of commissioned responses, by thirteen poets and the musician/composer Bill Frisell, to a sequence of eight abstractions by the painter Gerhard Richter.

Library of Congress Cataloging-in-Publication Data
Palmer, Michael, 1943–
Company of moths / Michael Palmer.
   p. cm.
ISBN 0-8112-1623-3 (alk. paper)
I. Title.
PS3566.A54C66   2005
811'.54—dc22   2005000994

New Directions Books are published for James Laughlin
by New Directions Publishing Corporation
80 Eighth Avenue, New York 10011

Company of Moths

Contents

3. COMPANY OF MOTHS

4. DREAM

"Enter the kingdom of words as if you were deaf."

—Carlos Drummond de Andrade

STONE

And

The ship—what was her name, its name?
Was it The Moth? Or The Moth
that Electrifies Night? Or The Moth

that Divides the Night in Half
in its Passage toward the Fire?
The fire of forgetting, that is,

as we remember it,
while in the scatter song of dailiness
as it eddies out

near turns to far, beeches, red cedars and oaks
dating to the revolution, and a few long before,
suddenly in unison are seen to fall,

for so somewhere it is writ.
And your project abandoned in fragments
there beneath the elements,

the snow of the season enfolding it,
the flames of the season consuming it,
improving it: Hashish, the tales it

tells, the scented oils and modern festivals,
the sphinx-like heads and the shining ornaments
for ankle, waist, neck and wrist,

dioramas, cosmoramas, pleoramas
(from *pleo*, "I sail," "I go by water"),
the hierophant in wax, the iron and glass,

the artificial rain and winds,
mosaic thresholds, all of this
bathed from above in diffuse light.

We share the invisible nature of these
things, our bodies and theirs.
And the moon did not appear that night.

to the memory of a suicide

Of

Of this photograph no one has taken

Eyes both a veil and sexual organ
The play as they always say

of light against shadow
first light then shadow then the shadow-play

Is it in color or black and white?

Yes it is in color or black and white

There are leaves drifting down,
a tiny skiff prepared to embark

across the waters of a painter's studio
toward a tower of clouds beyond the glass

The scatter of things

the room choking on pages
and the torn remnants of pages

No one to answer the telephone's ring
(Dearest Reader are there still phones still rings?)

They are afloat the two of them
in a sea of something

or perhaps they are drowning
or waiting for the wind to gather them up

into a palinode, a canticle, a stanza

If she has a question
will it go unasked?

(Are there still questions and questions unasked
Dearest Reader from the future-past?)

Berries brilliant orange on the hawthorn
this Wednesday late November

Blurred wing at the edge of the frame

Eyes unfocussed lost in her
thoughts as they always say

Eyes at once fixed and in motion

gilded aleph emerging from her mouth
mouth emerging from her mouth

So, it's claimed, an age begins

This photograph no one has seen
offers itself in evidence

The Thought

We breathe in, we do not think
of it. We walk and we speak

beneath the blue-flowering trees
and do not think. We breathe.

We cross the stone bridge
above a fisherman in a skiff.

We pass the blind man, the legless man
and the woman who sings of a coming storm.

We sit by the river in the rising wind,
we raise the crazed cup to our lips

and do not think,
here where the light does not differ from dark,

here where pages tumble to the floor,
here in the lake of ink, the stain of ink

where we fashion a calendar from a wall.
Invisible lake, unreachable shore.

Exhale and do not think.
Close their eyes a final time close our eyes.

to Faraj Bayrakdar

Stone

What of that wolfhound at full stride?
What of the woman in technical dress
and the amber eye that serves as feral guide

and witness
to the snowy hive?
What of the singer robed in red

and frozen at mid-song
and the stone, its brokenness,
or the voice off-scene that says,

Note the dragonfly by the iris
but ask no questions of flight,
no questions of iridescence?

All of this
and the faint promise of a sleeve,
the shuttle's course, the weave.

What of these?
What of that century, did you see it pass?
What of that wolfhound at your back?

Untitled (February 2000)

The naked woman at the window
her back to you, bowing the violin

behind the lace curtain
directly above the street

is not a fiction
as the partita is not a fiction

its theme and variations
ornaments and fills

not a fiction
as the one-way street still

wet from all this
rain is no fiction

and nakedness not a fiction.
It reads us like a book

as we listen to its music
through milky eyes wide shut.

And what does this fiction think of us?
The rain, the notes, both softly fall.

Slight errors of intonation do not matter
in the faded green

notebooks where we record these
things, and conceal other things.

What's the name of that tree, anyway,
with yellow flowers, small silver leaves,

planted in the concrete—
I used to know.

As for today, Leap Year Day,
the window was empty.

Untitled (July 2000)

The painter with no memory
paints the very thing

before him, this corner and its web,
this clock with its hands

frozen at five, neither day nor night.
Singing wordlessly

he paints the red and the green,
the shape, the sharpness of the thing,

the clear line of the lover's chin,
the one who will betray him.

He thinks: to pass through needle's eye.
Spiraling juniper, threaded, illegible

sky, arbutus past flower, groundsel,
wild columbine. And at the turn

of the breath it is so, and so:
It peers blindly through the eye,

it is white, not quite white
and is heard through the eye.

And the blossoming of dust,
phosphorescence of bones,

transfigured flight of geese.
The painter with no memory

paints the single thing
she sees, this ballast of stones,

ladder of mottled glass,
oval face, ashen-eyed, the dance

of the thing and its name,
lost limb and its shadow,

small paintings all of these,
each one the same.

The Turn (December 2000)

So it is the lift, the shifting of earth, the turn
So it is the pleasure of green, so simply,

we think, and the singing of stones
So it is the same mountain, yet otherwise—

yet not entirely otherwise,
slant logic of the half-torn, final leaf,

twig across a sickle moon
wobbling in the nightbreeze,

and your moment of wild speech, while dying
So the closing of eyes,

then the coining of eyes
What color were the eyes

So it is the same house
of wood and pitted tile,

ringing of keys, yet otherwise
It is the pleasure of things,

disappearance of things,
odd feel of those things

turned in the hand
this way and that,

remembered by the hand,
the winding of the steps,

turning of the page, the book
and setting the book to one side

and adjusting the light,
fiddling with the light,

setting of the book aside
It is a kind of memory of the book,

a blank book, edges cuffed,
book lying open and shut

Company of Moths

We thought it could all be found in The Book of Poor Text,
the shadow the boat casts, angled mast, fretted wake, indigo eye.

Windows of the blind text,
keening, parabolic nights.

And the rolling sun, sun tumbling
into then under, company of moths.

Can you hear what I'm thinking, from there, even as you sleep?
Streets of the Poor Text, where a child's gaze falls

on the corpse of a horse beside a cart,
whimpering dog, woman's mute mouth agape

as if to say, We must move on,
we must not stop, we must not watch.

For after all, do the dead watch us?
To memorize precisely the tint of a plum,

curve of a body at rest (sun again),
the words to each popular song,

surely that would be enough.
For are you not familiar with these crows by the shore?

Did you not call them sea crows once?
Did we not discuss the meaning of "as the crow flies"

one day in that square—station of exile—under the reddest
of suns? And then, almost as one, we said, It's time.

And a plate shattered, a spoon fell to the floor,
towels in a heap by the door.

Drifts of cloud over
steeples from the west.

Faith in the Poor Text.
Outline of stuff left behind.

Homage

"The rats outnumber the roses in our garden. That's why we've named it The Rat Garden."

A discussion of the sublime ensued. Aunt Klara served her ginger-peach tea. At ninety-six, many of her parts still worked. "It is life that should inspire fear, not death," she would say, quoting the Dietrich once again.

It was the first May Day of the new millennium, though no one could recall what that day meant. "Perhaps it is the day when the rat lies down with the rose," tiny Perdita remarked. All were aghast, as these were the first words she had ever uttered.

The skywriters were active that near windless day, their most frequent message, in cursive, "Rats Rule!" Slowly the letters would thicken and belly out toward the east, then dissolve into illegible smoke.

The sun declined; the mayflies made their entrance, and the sedulous bats.

Then the great evening feast was placed before us: pea soup with pork knuckle; the little *elver*, baby eels, almost transparent, quickly boiled and served with mashed turnip; and of course the goose, stuffed with Nuremberg sausage, chestnuts, onion, chopped carrot and cream; and finally a Black Forest cake, that baroque confection of chocolate, whipped cream, sweetened cherries and kirsch.

It was over coffee and brandy, as the evening drew to a close, that Uncle Johann suddenly blurted out, "I'm sorry, I know I'm a terrible poet." At that moment Perdita formed the second sentence of her inchoate life, "All poets know they are terrible."

Archive

Figures, what do they know
in those old books, asleep

in those brittle books? What do they dream
on the locked shelves, in The Book of Signs

and The Book of Delights, Queen Dido's book,
and the book we sought but couldn't find?

Bright archive, sad merriment,
those waters that once we bathed in,

spine against spine, their banks lined
with the smallest of flowers, pale blue.

Did you see them, darting beneath the eaves?
Hear them, right before night?

Should we share a breath or maybe two
with the ghost of the future, the slant rain,

the brindled rose, the keeper of the code?
What do they know

with their sealed lips, scattered limbs,
of the books that they rewrite?

Burning Deck

Therefore the choir, underneath
Therefore our work books, our waste books

and the dazzle of the streets, the rigged lotteries
and the too bright, speech-cancelling hours

Therefore the hand's thought, throat's thought
of promises and passages

singing ourselves away
(Can you hear the changes, can you,

first words, earliest, almost empty names,
tuned thread Adriana spins

up there at the dusty edge?)
And our bass player's from Montana

or Milwaukee, or some kinda smack
And so the tolling, the teeming shore

and the woman lying naked,
curled within the belly of an owl

We'd monitor her dreams if we could
across the starry night,

Good Ship Vertigo sliding through shadow,
blossoms of phosphor in its wake

Today, they claim, light has been brought to a stop
and stored, then sent upon its way

Therefore the bell bird, the clockwork carousel,
and the breath's turn—which way?

for Rosmarie and Keith

19

Tongue Asleep

A wind had cleared things out, stolen things. Had swept down the stair-well, it was that dark and late, dark field with swirling dots. Mass of summer stars, window shattered, all pages gone, all pens, all amulets, lists, all machines but one. How will you now read in the dark? asked the pyrographer. Where will you place your hands, how hold your arms? How hobble, how step from wall to wall? How gather in images forth-with? How focus the eyes, draw a comb through your hair, fix your gaze on the missing thing? How listen, where dwell? Once more, once more, said Khlebnikov. And that was all. Things were years. Idea of light, of flesh, of thought. Stolen things.

SCALE

The

The red vowels, how they spill
then spell a sea of red

And the bright ships—
are they not ghost ships

And the bridge's threads
against flame-scarred hills

And us outside
by other worlds

So

So the promise of happiness?
he asked a frog

then swallowed the frog
And the buzz of memory?

he asked the page
before lighting the page

And by night the sliding stars
beyond the night itself

A

A table erased
It is not realism makes possible the feast

Grey face turned away
Jam jar of forget-me-nots

Girl with gold chain
cinching her waist

But is it true
And what will become of us

As

As if the small voices—
one-erum two-erum

pompalorum jig
wire briar broken lock

then into and into
the old crow's nest—

and so when young,
before all the rest

Crease

Crease in the snowy field
of evening within us

How the owl stares
and startles there

fashioning mindless elegy
So the remembered world's

songs and flooded paths
This heap of photographs

This

This perfect half-moon
of lies in the capital

Crooks and fools in power what's new
and our search has begun for signs of spring

Maybe those two bluebirds
flashing past the hawthorn yesterday

Against that, the jangle of a spoon in a cup
and a child this day swept out to sea

But

But the birth and death of stars?
The birds without wings,

wings without bodies?
The twin suns above the harbor?

The accelerating particles?
The pools of spilled ink?

Pages turning themselves
in The Paper House?

Soon

Soon the present will arrive
at the end of its long voyage

from the Future-Past to Now
weary of the endless nights in cheap motels

in distant nebulae
Will the usual host

of politicians and celebrities
show up for the occasion

or will they huddle out of sight
in confusion and fear

COMPANY OF MOTHS

Folta la nuvola bianca delle falene impazzite
turbina intorno agli scialbi fanali sulle spallette . . .

Whirls the white cloud of mad moths
about the parapets' ashen lights . . .

—Montale, "La primavera hitleriana"

Pulse

Good to have a memory of silk,
memory of the glance, serene

and troubled all at once,
memory of the moth,

ghost moth or dog moth
flying upside down

between the possible and the what if,
the pulse and the confusion of limbs.

Letter to a Vagrant

Cupido, the frogs in our stomachs are singing as one.
Cupido, there are madeleines hanging in sacks, there's lava in Ghana,
each day new elephants on parade,

each night new slings, new arrows,
new weapons of mass affection,
so far from silence have we come.

And we no longer make out faces in the clouds,
Señor Cupido, or sails in the lengthening shadows.
Still, a mantis at least, pale green

on the garden wall this morning, now gone.
And our empty words continue to echo,
it seems, between the facing cliffs

even if there's no one left to hear them,
the tourists having long since departed
with their noise machines and extra-terrestrial clothes.

And our war against the mind
seems to be proceeding nicely,
and against the earth, Cupido,

all our ducks in a row,
profits surpassing forecasts,
light drizzle, sirens, and the first of the hyacinths.

So stop your growling,
stop scaring the children
and eat your bread soup

and wipe your mouth, Cupido,
prepare to board the burning boat
and sail forth, eyes closed.

Untitled (Three Days)

Yes, I changed the light bulb myself,
so no more jokes about poets and light bulbs,

or poets and light,
no more combing the unconscious

for its Corybantic folds, its flows,
and no more talk of "the bitter wind."

It will do what it must
to summon and confound

all at once
and ravel the wings of moths at dusk.

(Did we not, that same night,
carve the voice into parts

and number them one, then one plus one,
and so on?) Tea from the leaves of mint,

the tiny sisal boats, adrift
in shifting currents of air

as if elegy were endless.
Three days, one light bulb, now this.

Untitled (29 May 02)

So cut the rope, dusty ghost.
Time to leave, time to undream

the star charts and instruction books,
the smart cards and tootling teapots.

Remember that bogus Moscow map
they always handed out?

Remember the singer on stilts
in the mist by the Stone Bridge

raging against God and nakedness?
The plant sacred to Artemis,

a hairbrush abandoned beside it?
And the House of the Hanged Man

smelling of sage and mint?
Did you know, Capricorn is rising?

So pack up your favorite owls and goats
and barrel rolls, and let's go.

Apollinaire the Duck

One is amused by the tie, the hours and the clock,
the first hour, in which you gaze all around,
and the last, when you bounce up and down,

and the clock in your pocket becomes a watch.
I'd like to be a watch in your pocket,
counting the hours, the beats of the heart,

the muses at the doors of your body,
who make the hours stop.
Do you like my tie, my irregular heart

plucked from a drawer full of hearts
and that rack of a thousand ties
and ten-thousand stripes

peering out from the doleful dark
like a swarm of crazed butterflies, mad moths,
pursued by Dantean suicides

and frothing *philosophes*
toward a point of no return?
What if we reach that point

in the final hours of the clock,
casting off thoughts of the infinite,
will we have a good time?

Arc

There is the above and the below of each.
"Their wings . . . the lining underneath . . ."

There is our daily speech, so clear
and meaning-free. And meaning itself,

to be erased, almost successfully.
There is the red rose

and its double in the dark
avid to swallow us,

the dancing woman, many-armed,
in folds of cloth and gold,

and below, her silent counterpart,
undisclosed. The tree in full leaf

and the tree ablaze
are one we're told

by the riddling, riparian dream
(a dream I dreamt against the River Wye).

Do you remember how quiet
the skies became, that while,

before the clanging began again?
The wild poppies, their caps,

the sentinel owl,
the crescents and veining,

windrows and slopes?
Below they are tracing

an arc or enlacement
that can't be shown.

"No contrasts, no shading anymore . . ."
They are in the dark.

in memory of W.G. Sebald

The Dream of Narcissus

The dream of Narcissus,
that there would be a silence loud as time

The dream of the writer,
that there could be a silence loud as time

The dream of time,
that rest might come

The dream of rest,
that unrest might arise

The dream of the palm,
that pilgrims would enter the village

The dream of the village,
that they depart with their fronds

And the house dreaming of its leveling,
and the exile of his well

The dream of night,
that the day would be purified

The dream of day,
that the dark would be lifted

And the dream of the dream,
but who's to speak of this

The Phantom of Liberty

The summer snows, a bit of a surprise,
and the new turn our love-making has taken—

The Imam's Delight, The Secret Glyph, The Trial Balloon.
Why do such discoveries take so long?

We began, I remember, with the ordinary—
sips of juice, strips of bacon of a morning,

eggs over easy. So the decades passed
and pasture reverted to woodland

and the ghosts we thought long gone
returned, bearing fresh robes it's true,

and the sheep in the fields wandered up to the fence
and greeted them, come anew.

Snow coating the stone walls, the eaves, the little boat.
Snow on the wintergreen and the scarlet oak.

And the Emperors, Green Foresters, China Marks,
tracing and retracing their arcs

in the late, slant light.
And the ghosts with names and the ghosts with none.

The Triumph of Love

Its sadness is palpable, yet everywhere they assemble
in the folds of the marshes, the moraines and clefts.

And the street-pageant now, winding past the apothecary
as once it was known, the bank's proleptic façade,

Mylene's For Hair, the One Stop Party Shop,
Felisberto—Master of Chocolate.

Hello dancers and amputees,
legislators and hierophants,

financiers, makers of the masque.
How bodies multiply is not our business here,

nor how their faces glow in this light,
nor how they tell their tales, worshipping electrons

and brilliant sunsets all at once.
Nor the enigma of the sudden return

of the fireflies, beneath the Archer and the Swan,
and the Gorgon slayer, his array.

After all, we are not alone in dreaming at night,
and these dreams seem to have their own life

we can know little about. They call
back and forth, do they not,

somewhat outside of time?
Did we at last find our way?

Did the glare bother us?
And what of the fields of rye grass, near knee-high,

and Naseer's lute
that's neither you nor I?

The Merle Asleep

Asked the Merle, of Sleep,
Are you the kingdom of sand or the blessèd moon?

Asked the Merle, asleep,
Who are these blindered travelers

choiring Amazing Grace, Haunted Heart,
All the Things You Are,

while I can only speak
of thimbleberry, limestone and wheat,

of power lines and poles and shattered oaks
though I'd prefer by far to sing,

I who can only speak?
Said the Merle, fearing sleep,

I am the color of deep night
and I fear what night will bring,

its stuttered cries and moans,
its silences too loud and too complete,

the black ploughed night
far from waking life.

Asked the Merle, of Sleep,
Have you not noticed

how the notes fall through air
onto earth's clotted ears,

how there's no path leading up
to this gate rusted shut,

how the station pulls away
as the train draws near?

Said Sleep,
What the passengers are dreaming

I cannot tell.
You saw that newly minted sun

without horizon, that pit
of twined and mounded limbs,

that city with no center,
saw how the pines bent, stones shifted,

and the river was torn from its course,
saw how the living and the lost

breathe in helpless unison,
dancing their fevered reel.

The Words

The birds with bones of glass:
perhaps the terror will end

in a flowering tree in July.
The book lying open in the light,

the book with mottled spine,
all possible information inside:

Riemann hypothesis resolved,
the zeta and zeros, entry 425;

The Paradox of the Archer
on the succeeding page;

the lost language of moths
a little further along.

Slow wing beats of owls
down the book's corridors.

Sky a cadmium yellow
from the fires to the north.

They seem to follow us, the fires,
as page follows page.

The bones, the birds, the glass, the light, the primes;
book, words, zeros, fires, spine.

Sonnet: After Maurice Scève

How they wobble, the days, when she says,
You are meaner than time, much smaller than space.

And who will write this for me, in
my place, who'll witness the endless events

of mourning and remembrance?
That fevered song—I cannot hear it.

That cobalt drawing—cannot see it—
the one of mountains and moths,

a lantern alight. Who will write this,
the dream of the sea and its guests, the dancers

of diffracted light, the way they alter
each other's breath

in an eddy of limbs? How they wobble,
the days and the hours, this night.

Este Mundo

This world
with its sounds

and that other with its othering
where words then solid things

melt into sounds.

Enough?

This writing inside
the lids of the eyes.

Enough?

This table enough,
these wars enough?

A sip enough,
a glimpse?

Oars spinning,
the broken notes enough,

the drunken boats?

And the idol asleep in the mountain,
his nurse's milk on his lips.

He's dreaming of peacocks,
meteors, pyromanic moths,

dreaming of serpents and pyramids,
worlds hanging from clouds,

the wine jug, the lover's spine,

and fire as it claims
the edges of a page.

Bastante?

This world
in the fold of an echo:

You can hear them
beneath the mown field,

the restive songs.

for Pura López-Colomé

Jackal and Falcon

O Gerardo Deniz, tell me, if you know,
is it only pyruvic acid

that causes the Muses' tears to flow?
And who was Galatea anyway?

(Someone asked me yesterday.)
And the map as large as a territory,

whose thing is that?
And that the map is blank,

a perfect whiteness as of sand,
sand that whistles and shifts?

And the cities beneath that sand,
the canopic jars, the fractured tablets?

(Four sons had Horus: baboon,
human, jackal and falcon.)

And the Forbidden Rice, deep indigo,
of which we are so often told,

its grains as dark as pages are light,
is it ever to be known

and rolled upon the tongue?
Or is it only to be sung?

It's suddenly gotten cold. I'm putting on
my stolen sweater and this coat.

Untitled (October 2002)

Eva Braun advised me in a dream
to always be kind to dogs.

So I gazed at the world
with fresh eyes, the rust

on the apple, the sliding sun,
our hard-won freedoms here at home.

Then a famous physicist proudly proclaimed
that this century would be no less

exciting than the last—
not a dream. So I set a match

to my *Obras Completas*, all thirteen pages,
that sad house of paper,

and let loose the finch from its cage.
Next a woman in red, not undressing, said,

Stop playing the flaming fool.
But how exactly is that done?

So I summoned my dog,
name of Bob, gnarly dog,

tossed him a glabrous bone,
told him he was not alone.

Untitled (December 2002)

And so this book of all the words
and their doubles. We welcome the words
for zero and for one,

for sleep and for space
and their doubles. Of the others
we're not so sure.

We welcome silence and the arcs,
the half-light, the cavalcade,
sorrows of the moon and the sun,

none of the above.
Magpies by the Tam—remember?
Said the one:

I'm burning now, I'm burning up
and still the river runs.
Said the double:

O little book,
enormous, empty book,
the woman and the bird and the man

were never one.
It was a mistake, maybe of the eye.
And this allée of pepper trees

is not endless.
And the book.
The winter day is endless.

Untitled (February 2003)

It's true that sometimes I've used the word raisin in place of reason,
true that I'm surprised each time

by the sudden progress of the seasons
and that often when all is said

all comes undone. Look at how the worms
turned into gods

before our filmy eyes
and how the lyric

war machine sings
in the greyness of the morning.

And the name of its song?
But here we are

among the dogs large and small
of the afterdawn.

Is it possible to make love in such light
or read from the first pages of Silence?

The bright, early butterflies
at Pura's place, under the volcano.

Campesinos blockading the roads.
Es bueno.

Vamos viver . . .

Of the paradise that was not,
no one can speak.

Of the place that was,
no one can speak.

Of the owl and the moth,
of the breeze up north.

Of the scorpion and the millipede,
of the windrows of straw,

flecked iris of the eye.
Of the rodents who rule

In the Name of the Lord.
Of the after all and the overall,

the was and because.
The shadow, the wheel of absence,

the past of each space.
So let's drop it all

and head up north
where at least there's a breeze.

after Bandeira

The Turn (May 2003)

What is that turn you took in Beltà, in Beauty?
A blind man is staring out at the sea,

the waves, their foaming crests—
Abed those songs—

and what of the fog that forgives
or only pretends?

That turn, the slight angle of the head,
the wild berries, those to be eaten,

these not. Could you, could anyone
have known it would come to this—

the fragments and chants,
that ringing

that in Beltà, in Beauty
tethers and unties,

embraces and shoves aside?
And the fumblings, the bright, unraveling threads,

the taste that lingers in the mouth,
that turn at last toward *far*.

Too many hours in the poem.
Last one left awake once again.

Una Noche

Then El Presidente,
uncoiling his tongue,

"You cannot stop time
but you can smash all the clocks."

And so, seeking Paradise,
we have burned the bright house

to the ground.
A necessary act.

We have invented glass
and ground a dark lens

and in the perilous night
we continue to dance.

The tarantella, the tango,
the passadoble and the jig,

the bunnyhop, the Cadillac,
the Madison and sarabande,

mazurka and the jerk,
the twist on tabletops.

Rolling our eyes,
flailing our limbs.

It's how we keep time,
our feet never stop.

Hive

Listen—but who's listening?
It's 2067 who's listening?

It's yesterday who is listening
right then, and night, last night

or the next, beneath its lamp,
its guttering light, tiny arc,

day fast gone who's speaking
from the future-past,

speaking in the roar
and the watery streets,

the transparent night, that
hive of woven glass,

a diver caught within?
And the chemist at his bench

at work on the problem of rust,
the problem of memory,

problem of cadmium dust,
problem of the future-past.

He thinks, In liquid things dissolve,
I saw a diver in a hive

of woven glass, a cloud, a filigree.
Who speaks who listens who hears or sees?

But they have fallen

But they have fallen to the ground
amid the twigs and leaves

all dry. And we bend
to pick them up, these things,

we think to pick them up
but we cannot

hard as we try.
It is too dark or else too light.

There's been a failure at the source of light,
a fractured moon or swollen sun,

and our fingers one by one
have grown numb.

My Lecture

My lecture. It began in dreams,
the topics merging.

Painters and dancers,
I've forgotten your names

as you have mine.
We were there together

in that vast room,
and the rent was due.

We moved cautiously,
so as not to offend.

We spoke in the end,
sotto voce, of the gates

we must pass through
and the ruins beyond,

motion as time,
gesture as light,

the fracturing patterns,
all those fictions and fears

and the years,
rent still due.

Your Diamond Shoe

Don't write poems about what's going on.
Murderers and liars, dreams and desires,

they're always going on.
Leave them outside the poem.

Don't describe your sad-eyed summer home
or wide-eyed winter home.

Don't write about being homeless
or your home-away-from-home.

Don't write about war,
whether you're against or for,

it's the same fucking war.
Don't talk about language,

don't talk about loss.
Don't mention truth or beauty

or your grandpa's bones.
No one wants to know

how your father/brother/lover
deducted himself. Razor, rope or gun,

what's the difference?
Whisper nothing of the snow

on the Contrescarpe,
nothing of moths, their fluttering arcs,

or the towers—how we watched them fall.
Don't write at all.

after Drummond

Night Gardening

A reader writes to complain
that there are no cellphones in my poems,
so here is one,

its body chrome,
its face a metallic blue.
It's neither transmitting nor receiving.

A woman from Duluth requests
that I cease sending secret messages
to her in my poems.

This I will do forthwith.

And the blackbird at evening.

She says, You have misrepresented the river
there where it turns

by the holm oak and the bed
of winter hyacinths.

This I will correct.

A recent letter unsigned:
You've mangled the citations from Hölderlin,

and none will mistake your skies
for those of Dominikos Theotokopoulos.

Opines a good citizen, concerned parent,
Your nefarious syntax
has infected my first-born—

have you a heart of stone?

And the poem, from its homeless home,
writes of blindsight and silence,

the blackbird at evening,
nothing you can see.

Finisterrae

The eye on each wing, for example,
many have mentioned this.

That it sees nothing,
no one has mentioned this.

The Classical Study

I asked the Master of Shadows
wherefore and wherefrom

but he said that art was short
and life was long

Said: let us praise
those flames that consume the day

stone by stone
and the lilac by the barn

and the hours when you were young
and the mother- and the father-tongue.

Curled by fire the leaves of grass,
buckled, the roof beam,

shattered, the wagon's haft,
ash-flecks in the wind's swell.

Have you forgotten the whistling of the stones,
the heave and shift of the windrows?

So I asked the Master of Shadows
about the above and the below,

the this and the that,
the first and the last,

but he said,
I am no master

only a shadow,
and he laughed.

DREAM

Have we learned how to waltz through hell,
imitate the silence of the bells?

Dream of a Language that Speaks

Hello Gozo, here we are,
    the spinning world, has

it come this far?
    Hammering things, speeching them,

nailing the anthrax
    to its copper plate,

matching the object to its name,
    the star to its chart.

(The sirens, the howling machines,
    are part of the music it seems

just now, and helices of smoke
    engulf the astonished eye;

and then our keening selves, Gozo,
    whirled between voice and echo.)

So few and so many,
    have we come this far?

Sluicing ink onto snow?
    I'm tired, Gozo,

tired of the us/not us,
    of the factories of blood,

tired of the multiplying suns
    and tired of colliding with

the words as they appear
    without so much as a "by your leave,"

without so much as a greeting.
The more suns the more dark—

is it not always so—
and in the gathering dark

Ghostly Tall and Ghostly Small
making their small talk

as they pause and they walk
on a path of stones,

as they walk and walk,
skeining their tales,

testing the dust,
higher up they walk—

there's a city below,
pinpoints of light—

high up they walk,
flicking dianthus, mountain berries,

turk's-caps with their sticks.
Can you hear me? asks Tall.

Do you hear me? asks Small.
Question pursuing question.

And they set out their lamp
amid the stones.

for Yoshimasu Gozo